INTUITION OF AN INTROVERT

DEEPIKA PONUGOTI

Made with ♥ on the Notion Press Platform
www.notionpress.com

This book is dedicated to my parents, Almighty and all the wonderful people who supported me to read more and more, write more and more, tapped on my shoulders and motivated me to power it up every time, when I felt low.

To my lovely daughter Samanvitha, I love you to the moon and back and this would be the precious and proud gift that I can ever give you. Your mother is an author now!!!

Contents

Contents

Foreword

Yes, I am an introvert! And here is my intuition in a nutshell!!!

I prefer abstract subjects over lengthy conversations!

I prefer authenticity over elegance!

I look at the bigger picture than every minute detail!

Shout out to all the introverts! Stop scrolling the screen and start scrolling the pages and don't let yourself down. You are amazing just the way you are!!!

Preface

This book is a collection of my emotions in the form of words expressing my sorrow, grief and happiness. Being an introvert is the first step towards becoming a great poet because books become your best friends and travelling through the path of your imagination would be your guilty pleasure. I am a normal woman searching for happiness by reading between the lines and writing down my thoughts.

Acknowledgements

I would like to express my deepest sense of gratitude to all the wonderful people who chose to read my poems and write-ups. This means world to me!

Prologue

Feeling happy? Read this book and smile
Feeling sad? Read this book and smile

1. **** I WISH ****

*I wish you knew that I may forgive but I will never forget what
happened to me
I wish you wouldn't have said that you need a person
like me for the rest of your life*

*I wish we never had our first kiss and first love which ended up
in vain
I wish you were clear with your decisions and haven't portrayed
that you're confused*

*I wish you have been able to understand and had respect for my
feelings
I wish you never turned back and repeated the same old fake
chapter of our story again and again*

*I wish you stood by me when I needed you the most and your eyes
never lied
I wish you were genuine and honest enough to tell me that things
won't work out for us*

*I rock to the eager rhythms and dip into sultry voices and being
drenched in the burden of emotions, I WISH ... Yes i strongly*

WISH!!!

2. **** DITCH THE LABELS ****

Why do we put labels on people?

Of course, it helps us feel safe and superior but it silently KILLS us.

From a cheesy pick up line, "Tu cheeez badi hai masth" to "She's too hot to handle"

From a popular saying, "Mard ko kabhi dar nahin hota" to "Men will be men"

From a superstitious perception, "Ladke rote nahin" to "You are too timid being a man"

From a disappointing compliment, "You're not like other women, you do less drama" to "You, being a woman know a lot about latest technology, that's a surprise"

From making obnoxious remarks on the external appearance using phrases like "that fat lady, that dark woman, that bald-headed person, that skinny girl, that short guy" to making funny names based on their disabilities like "that squint-eyed guy, that absent minded girl"

We put labels on people to differentiate artificially judging their natural behavior and characteristics, thus humiliating them to irreparable extent

Labels are messy; Some may be positive conveying something absolute, while some may disrupt the confidence of people who are being victimized by labels
Let's start tossing labels aside and start to cement the assumption that it's completely fine to have an average life. Chasing perfection to gain happiness is a myth.

3. **** DON'T ASSUME, ASK YOURSELF ****

Instead of assuming, "I'm so fat, I should starve myself again", Have you ever tried asking yourself, "I haven't been taking care of myself properly, Can I be more gentle and kind with my body?"

Instead of assuming, "No one likes me", Have you tried asking yourself, "Do I need to please everyone?"

Instead of assuming, "I am not smart enough", Have you ever tried asking yourself, "Did I even try or, have I given my best shot yet?"

Instead of assuming, "I am an airhead", Have you ever tried asking yourself, "Did I realize that with time and exposure, I will be more comfortable?"

Instead of assuming, "I am a bad friend", Have you ever tried asking yourself, "Did I respond to my friends right away, when they've texted me?"

Instead of assuming, "My home is always untidy and unorganized", Have you ever tried asking yourself, "Did I try to declutter and keep only what sparks joy?"

Instead of assuming, "I'm irresponsible", Have you ever tried asking yourself, "Can I learn to prioritize better?"

Instead of assuming, "I'm not beautiful", Have you ever tried asking yourself, "Am I brave and bold enough to accept my flaws and scars and still, be kind to myself?"

You don't deserve to hit your sheets every night, feeling depressed and worthless!!! Love yourself!

4. **** GOD IS BAD AT MATH ****

God is bad at math; he doesn't know how to answer the prayers based on the level of honesty

God is bad at math; he doesn't know how to grant wisdom based on the level of maturity

God is bad at math; he doesn't know how to help us find the light at the end of dark cave

God is bad at math; he doesn't know how to take us into His arms when in anguish and plague

God is bad at math; he doesn't know how to heal the grief when in torment and bane

God is bad at math; he doesn't know how to give an extra dose of happiness when in pain

Yet, God has the superpower to ensure the happening of miracles beyond the logic of math;

5. **** HOLD ON ****

From trying to fit in, to fall in and out, we must hold on.
From asking for a reason, to let go of explanation, we must hold
on.

From being happy, to being a people pleaser, we must hold on.
From being strong, to being peaceful, we must hold on.

From being a fighter, to being a loner, we must hold on.
We would have if we could have. Only time does it for us and
we accept it knowingly or unknowingly.

Give time to time because it truly is THE healer.

6. **** LOSER ****

*You're not a loser if you give your opinion and others strike down
and disagree with you*

*You're not a loser if you are in calm waters when others start to
throw tantrums on you*

*You're not a loser when you're crippled inside and still manage to
carry a smile on you*

*You're not a loser when you accept your flaws even if others say, I
pity you*

*You're not loser if you don't fall under the scope of flattering and
fascinating praise*

*You're not a loser if you are fundamentally honest not to accept
the hypocrisy and move on*

*You're not a loser if you don't become famous on social media at
a faster pace*

*You're not a loser if you don't live a luxurious life or don't get
married in your early 30's*

*You're not a loser if someone doesn't accept you saying that you're
not good enough for them*

You're not a loser if you can't become a hashtag and asterisk trend

Living a happy and peaceful life with contentment is a blessing

*You're a loser if you don't like and believe yourself and not
matured enough to unlove yourself when you're wrong and*

restart loving yourself when you're right
You're a loser if you refuse to get up, dress up and show up your
strength whenever you fall down
You're a loser if you're always a follower instead of being an
influencer
You're a loser if you keep aside your identity and behave different
just to impress others
You're a loser when you blame yourself for everything in your life
instead of seeking a solution

7. **** MEMORIES ****

Life is full of memories, good, bad and worse, most of them entwined into the gyri and sulci of our brain, repeatedly flashing through our subconscious mind, even if the instances are gone forever. Some of them are captured by our camera, beautifully framed and archived in our phones, that are impossible to reproduce and the rest by our nocturnal senses, which make us become addicted to the pleasure of not losing them ever.

It's the moments that make memories, not the places and dates. Some of them tickle our cheeks and bring a smile, while a few are filled with guilt and distress, making our eyes wet and the heart heavier.

Some memories keep us haunting day and night, while some of them force us to turn the page or simply close it. However, they always run through the mind, rise in the heart and gather to the eyes, enduring the beautiful burden of the past.

One quick memory that goes by your mind can make your day, while it's hard to catch it and make it stay for a while. At that point, we all wish to have an intelligent system to track where it is in time, repeat, and replay whenever we want to. Yet, it's ironic how we remember few memorable moments and narrativise ourselves like professional novelists.

I believe that everyone will cast their net into the memories, someday or the other walking into the past virtually with a key of happiness in their pockets, trying to unlock their favorite and fond memories.

Some memories are distorted without a clear distinction between facts and events, while some are clearly captured as immutable and static possessions. Some may find it difficult to remember everything after a while struggling to reconstruct and emphasize their good memories, while some may try so hard to get rid of the bad memories and end up burying them in the corner of their mind, locked and lost.

Good or bad, small or big, happy or sad, temporary or permanent, memories always have been a topic of fascination, that excite us with a recombinative power of thought, making them eternal and eloquent. If you ask me how rich I am, I can narrate my memories worth millions of dollars and still counting.

During these difficult times of lockdown, it is essential to rewire our brain with refreshing memories and energize ourselves with the happiness brought by the moments that make us smile and feel happy all the day along. Rush into your past, find your memories and I wish you all a memorable evening ahead !!!

8. **** MIRROR ****

*How do you define your mirror? To, me my Mirror is my
Doppelganger*

*I don't know if the hips don't lie (I will leave it to Shakira) but
my mirror doesn't lie to me.. NEVER...!!!*

*When I'm happy, it shows me three times more beautiful than
how my face looks usually, in reality*

*When I'm sad, it reminds me that the tears are rolling down the
cheeks and I need to wipe them off and become stubbornly
resilient*

*When people judge me with obnoxious parade of hate words, it
reminds me that I am a better person than what they think*

*When people praise me, it pulls me down to ground saying, there
is a long way to go and you need to work harder*

*People love, people leave and people let you down, but your
mirror doesn't*

*People try, people lie and people can't look straight into your eyes,
but your mirror doesn't*

*People dare, people scare and people tell you what to wear, but
your mirror doesn't*

*My mirror doesn't get tired of showing the real and raw version
of me, no matter how many times I look into it*

Even if I break it into thousands of pieces, it doesn't stop showing my reflection in every broken piece of it. Love it.. I just love it..

9. **** PICK UP LINES

****

Do you have 11 protons? Because you are sodium fine!!

Do you have a nickname or, should I call you mine?

Are you a pick up line because I keep googling you!!

Your intelligence and my face, our babies will be great!!

Aren't you tired because you're constantly running in my head!!

Did it hurt, when you fell from heaven?

Are you Wi-Fi because I feel connected??

Hey! Are you a needle? because you have punctured my heart!!

Did your license get suspended for driving all these guys crazy??

Do you like raisins? How about a date instead??

Are you Paris? because Eiffel for you!!

Is your name Gillette? Because you are best a man can get!!

So, aside from taking my breath away, what do you do for a living??

I'd say God bless you but it looks like he already did!!

10. **** CONDITIONS APPLY ****

When a merciless mind gives you love, conditions apply that your heart may be broken
When a selfish soul offers you advice, conditions apply that your peace would be stolen

When someone has their own priorities, conditions apply that you may be taken for granted
When everyone laughs at your lame pun, conditions apply that most of them didn't get what you said

When people spend time with you when you need, conditions apply that you may ignore them and run
When someone gives a compliment without a reason, fakeness alert, take an above turn

When time-bound affection hits you all of a sudden, conditions apply that it's just for fun
When you are bored of too much of their honesty, conditions apply that they leave and never return

*When you feel lonely and think of someone, conditions apply
that they would surely make you cry*

*When you are connected to someone but have someone else in
mind, conditions apply that one must be true and other would
be a lie*

*Even an unconditional love is bound to some conditions with a
heavy being.. So never trust blindly and yet never give up so
easily*

11. **** THAT GIRL ****

THAT Girl, who has experienced a verbal abuse in childhood with a hateful and hurtful barrage of words, is now feeling worthless and battling depression

THAT Girl, whose teenage brain was plagued with labels of being ugly and disgusting, is now imprisoned in thoughts of being a meaningless molecule in existence

THAT Girl, who was molested at a tender age, has now morphed into an introvert, wrapping herself in a shroud of shyness, hiding from the world to protect herself

THAT Girl, who was bullied for being too heavy to be loved or even to be happy, is now starving herself for days, to the brink of exhaustion and crippling pain, praying if it was enough to be thin

THAT Girl, who has been cheated in relationship multiple times, has now lost trust in human beings, struggling hard to get rid of overthinking and low self-esteem issues

THAT Girl, who lost her loved ones, is now trying to conquer her mental illness and settling herself free from those dark times

DON'T BE THAT GIRL !!!!

Attention is temporary, but mental illness is real. Love your imperfections, #wabi-sabi, because anxiety and depression, whatever the name you give it, it all lies in your head. It's not a bruise or wound to be visible on skin and yet much more dangerous than you think it is!
Break the stereotypes, it is completely fine to be imperfect!

12. **** LET'S NORMALIZE ****

- Same sex parents and they/them pronouns -

- Feminine boys and masculine girls -

- People wearing whatever they want regardless of gender -

- Breaking down and showering grief -

- Not being strong all the time -

- Not being practical and questioning the norm -

- Men wearing makeup and crying when in pain -

- Finding love in 40s and chasing dreams in 30s

- Let's normalize having boundaries and standing up for ourselves!!!

13. **** IT'S OKAY ****

Do you sometimes feel happy if someone ignores you? - It's Okay

Do you feel numb when the situation demands a better reaction from you? - It's Okay

Do you remain silent assuming that words don't always do what they're meant to? - It's Okay

Do you feel bad for petty issues and overthink about it even if it's not necessary ? - It's Okay

Do you fall short of words and hesitate to talk properly in front of your special ones? - It's Okay

Do you sometimes avoid expressing your feelings properly ? - It's Okay

Do you feel low but you try to mask your emotions by wearing a smile ? - It's Okay

ACTIONS SPEAK MORE THAN WORDS
If someone can understand your silence and accept you the way you are, words don't need a room !!!

14. **** PAUSE and REFLECT ****

** When we are young, learning can be hard,*
*And mastery of intelligence could be an art**

**When we are grown up, it must be realized,*
*We should neither be bullied nor criticized**

** Some are older when they find their potential,*
*Some are young and well taught it is essential**

** Some people go through a lot not having a clue,*
*What is right, what is wrong and what they must do**

** Don't put pressure on things that aren't easy,*
*Life brings you to the place you deserve to be**

** Pause and reflect on your thoughts everyday*
*We are normal human beings that's all I can say**

15. **** AFRAID TO LOVE AGAIN ****

They said, her heart was as hard as stone.
And her emotions were as cold as ice.

Her face was clueless and she seldom smiles
But when she smiles, it is elusive,
As elusive as her dream to love again.

She is afraid, afraid to love and afraid to smile.
She feared the word LOVE, she can't hear the word
LOVE

Because she was scared that in the end,
She would get hurt again.

16. **** BRUTAL FACTS
**** 

Stop chasing the wrong ones, the right ones won't run away from you

Your obsession with finding happiness is what prevents its attainment

You can't make everyone happy, and if you try, you'll lose yourself

You can't be perfect, holding yourself to unrealistic standards creates suffering

If someone takes you for granted, blame yourself for allowing them to do so

It is not what happens that bothers, but how you react actually matters

Fame is temporary and fleeting, stop chasing fireworks and start building constellation

It is worth giving your time to someone only if it creates a good memory to yourself

17. **** LOOK AT YOU ****

Look at you, you have learned how to contemplate your priorities
Look at you, you have learned how to heal yourself amidst the crippling circumstances
Look at you, you have learned how to read between the lines and analyze accordingly
Look at you, you have learned how to respond to the negativity with a smile on your face
Look at you, you have learned to say NO and really mean it when you actually say it
Look at you, you have learned how to tell people politely to exit from your life, in order to make peace
Look at you, you have stopped wasting your time and emotion on someone who doesn't really care about you
Look at you, you have realized that existence is much more important than acceptance
Look at you, you have started taking decisions based on your vulnerability and willingness
LOOK AT YOU, YOU ARE SMILING, YOU ARE HEALING AND YOU ARE SURVIVING

18. **** ARE YOU JUST MY BESTIE? ****

My friend, we've been together
From the beginning till the end
Like that night stars till sun dawn
You provided me with a home inside you, am never alone.
Despite the distance
Despite the differences
God brought us to one another
I will cherish you in my heart forever
Thank you for being there
For being a friend whom I will always remember.
With you I have the dexterity to bounce back
From adversity and create oneself anew
So allow me to call you my best friend
For you played an important role in my life
I forever need you and I like you to the moon and back
Because you are the light I need in my journey.
You are a part of my past
And together we will be to the last
Without you I bet I would be lost
So I will treasure you at whatever cost

It's been laughter after laughter
With you, I pray we are friends even in the hereafter.
Friends unless when it is dark
Friends are there when you shine
Like staring God from above
I will be there when you need me
Although friendship is about risking life
My spine will double yours
To keep you going

19. **** DID THAT STOP? ****

Did that Indian matchmaker stop judging your profile based on your profile picture?

Did that neighbor stop suggesting you home remedies to improve your complexion?

Did that-so-called relative aka well-wisher stop insulting you for choosing bright colors to wear?

Did that judgmental guy/girl stop laughing at you because you are confident in your own skin?

Did that favorite celebrity of yours stop endorsing fairness creams/brands?

Did that famous actress stop herself from improving the shade of her epidermis?

Did that popular fairness brand stop asking you to mask your flaws by icing your skin with their cream?

Finally, did you stop consulting cosmetologist to peel that unwanted shade of paint off from your face?

Did you stop taking pictures without filters just to become Insta-perfect?

Did you stop searching for profiles on matrimonial sites using the filter, FAIR?

Did you stop being yourself and afraid to step out (of course, not now) without makeup on?

Did you stop covering your insecurities with a brighter shade of foundation and a bold lip color?

IF NOT, MY DEAR KEYBOARD WARRIORS, please don't use the hashtag, "STOP RACISM"

Be real, Be yourself and Be a person of purpose!!!

20. **** TOGETHER FOREVER ****

I always asked you if you had a special one, You smiled and replied saying there's no one

You said that you don't want to fall in love, Maybe you don't know the meaning of love

If it's for your happiness, I'm here to support you, That's the love I have for you

You don't want to close that door, for the friendship we had, even though we find someone else for a greater good or bad

We treat each other like more than a friend, Together and forever until the end

21. **** NEW BEGINING ****

- Maybe if we start over again with a new hope it would be different

- Maybe this time we will know and understand the mistakes before they happen

- Maybe we will realize the consequences and remember what caused them

- Maybe we will clearly see the love inside of unnoticed warm gestures of our loved ones

- May we see the beauty that is bestowed in kindness and gentleness like the noon day sun

- Maybe we can talk about the things we kept hidden and spend more time together

- Maybe we could restore what was lost and our love won't be fair-weathered

****If we start over again it would be different***
-Let's learn from the past, let's enjoy the essence of present and let's pray for a better future

Thank You